CGP

GCSE
Maths Buster

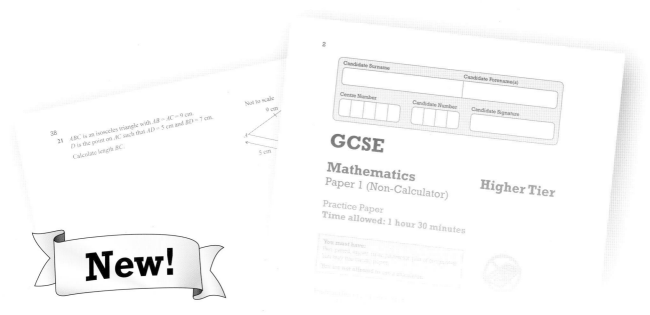

New!

Mock Exam Papers

For the Grade 9-1 Course — Higher Level

GCSE
Maths *Buster*

This book contains all three of the GCSE practice papers
from the Higher Level version of CGP MathsBuster.

You'll find step-by-step solutions and mark schemes
in the 'Mock Exams' section of MathsBuster
— you can print them out or view them on screen.

Mock Exam Papers
Higher Level

Contents

Published by CGP

Editors: Rob Harrison, Shaun Harrogate, David Ryan.
Contributor: Alastair Duncombe.
With thanks to Simon Little for the proofreading.

Clipart from Corel®
Printed by Elanders Ltd, Newcastle upon Tyne

Formulas in the Exams

GCSE Maths uses a lot of formulas — that's no lie. You'll be scuppered if you start trying to answer a question without the proper formula to start you off. Thankfully, CGP is here to explain all things formula-related.

You're Given these Formulas

Fortunately, those lovely, cuddly examiners give you some of the formulas you need to use.

> **For a sphere radius *r*, or a cone with base radius *r*, slant height *l* and vertical height *h*:**
>
> **Volume of sphere** $= \frac{4}{3}\pi r^3$ **Volume of cone** $= \frac{1}{3}\pi r^2 h$
>
> **Surface area of sphere** $= 4\pi r^2$ **Curved surface area of cone** $= \pi rl$

And, actually, that's your lot I'm afraid. As for the rest...

Learn All The Other Formulas

Sadly, there are a load of formulas which you're expected to be able to remember straight out of your head. There isn't space to write them all out below, but here are the highlights:

Compound Growth and Decay:
$$N = N_0\left(1 + \frac{r}{100}\right)^n$$
where N = total amount, N_0 = initial amount, r = percentage change and n = number of days/weeks/years etc.

The Quadratic Equation:
The solutions of $ax^2 + bx + c = 0$, where $a \neq 0$
$$x = \frac{-b \pm \sqrt{(b^2 - 4ac)}}{2a}$$

Where $P(A)$ and $P(B)$ are the probabilities of events A and B respectively:

$$P(A \text{ or } B) = P(A) + P(B) - P(A \text{ and } B)$$
or: $P(A \text{ or } B) = P(A) + P(B)$ (If A and B are mutually exclusive.)

$$P(A \text{ and } B) = P(A) \times P(B \text{ given } A)$$
or: $P(A \text{ and } B) = P(A) \times P(B)$ (If A and B are independent.)

Area of trapezium $= \frac{1}{2}(a + b)h_v$

For a right-angled triangle:
Pythagoras' theorem: $a^2 + b^2 = c^2$
Trigonometry ratios:
$$\sin x = \frac{O}{H}, \quad \cos x = \frac{A}{H}, \quad \tan x = \frac{O}{A}$$

For any triangle *ABC*:

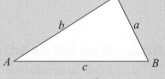

Sine rule: $\dfrac{a}{\sin A} = \dfrac{b}{\sin B} = \dfrac{c}{\sin C}$

Cosine rule: $a^2 = b^2 + c^2 - 2bc\cos A$

Area of triangle $= \frac{1}{2}ab\sin C$

Compound Measures:
$$\text{Speed} = \frac{\text{Distance}}{\text{Time}} \qquad \text{Density} = \frac{\text{Mass}}{\text{Volume}} \qquad \text{Pressure} = \frac{\text{Force}}{\text{Area}}$$

Candidate Surname		Candidate Forename(s)

Centre Number	Candidate Number	Candidate Signature

GCSE

Mathematics
Paper 1 (Non-Calculator)

Higher Tier

Practice Paper
Time allowed: 1 hour 30 minutes

You must have:
Pen, pencil, eraser, ruler, protractor, pair of compasses.
You may use tracing paper.

You are **not allowed** to use a calculator.

Instructions to candidates
- Use **black** ink to write your answers.
- Write your name and other details in the spaces provided above.
- Answer **all** questions in the spaces provided.
- In calculations show clearly how you worked out your answers.
- Do all rough work on the paper.

Information for candidates
- The marks available are given in brackets at the end of each question.
- You may get marks for method, even if your answer is incorrect.
- There are 20 questions in this paper. There are no blank pages.
- There are 80 marks available for this paper.

Get the answers
Worked solutions to this practice paper are available in PDF format, which you can print out
or view on screen. To find the solutions, go to the 'Mock Exams' section of MathsBuster.

Answer ALL the questions.

Write your answers in the spaces provided.

You must show all of your working.

1   A is 60% of B.
     B is 30% of C.

     What percentage of C is A? Circle the correct answer.

     18%   28%   30%   90%

[Total 1 mark]

---

2   Circle the graphs that match the following descriptions.

     (a)   A straight line has equation $y = mx + c$ where m > 0 and c < 0.

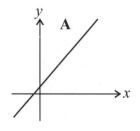 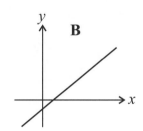 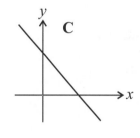 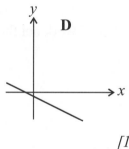

[1]

     (b) y is inversely proportional to x.

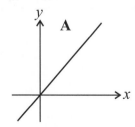 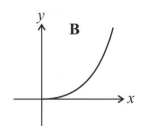 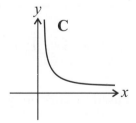 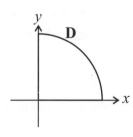

[1]

[Total 2 marks]

1

3 *ABCD* is a rectangular piece of card.

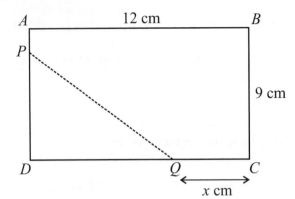

Not to scale

P is the point two-thirds of the way along *DA*.
Q is *x* cm from *C*.

The card is cut into two pieces along the line *PQ*.
The ratio of the areas of the smaller piece to the larger piece is 1 : 3

(a) Find the area of triangle *DPQ*.

.... cm²

[2]

(b) Work out the value of *x*.

x = ...

[3]

[Total 5 marks]

4 Estimate the value of

$$\sqrt[3]{\frac{785.3 \times 2.156}{0.1972}}$$

Show the numbers you used to work out your estimate.

....

[Total 3 marks]

5   The diagram shows a square *EFGH*.
The square has been divided into smaller squares and isosceles triangles.

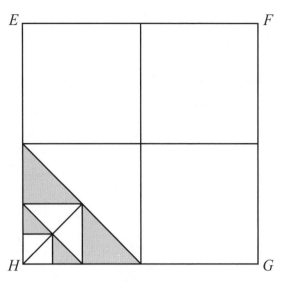

What fraction of the square *EFGH* has been shaded?

....

[Total 3 marks]

6   The *n*th term of a sequence is given by the formula $n^2 + 2n + 5$

(a) Fran says "The 4th term in the sequence is a prime number."
Is Fran correct? Tick a box.

Yes ☐   No ☐

Show how you worked out your answer.

....

....

[2]

(b) A different sequence begins   2, 5, 7, 12, 19, ...
Write down the next two terms in the sequence.

.... and ....

[2]

[Total 4 marks]

Paper 1 (non-calculator)

7 $\xi = \{1, 2, 3, \ldots, 10\}$
$A = \{x : 2 < x \leq 6\}$
$B = \{x : x \text{ is a factor of } 12\}$

Complete the Venn diagram to show the elements of each set.

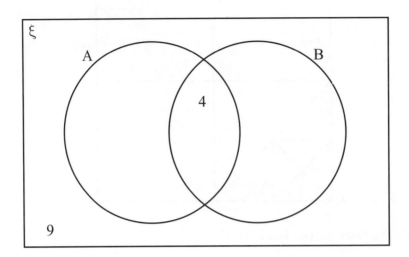

[Total 3 marks]

8   (a)   Find values of a and b such that $3a + 2b = 17$
$2a + b = 10$

$a = $ ....

$b = $ ....

[3]

   (b)   Hence, work out $a\begin{pmatrix} 2 \\ 1 \end{pmatrix} - b\begin{pmatrix} 3 \\ 2 \end{pmatrix}$

....

[2]

[Total 5 marks]

Paper 1 (non-calculator)

9 The scale drawing shows the position of three hospitals, *A*, *B* and *C*, on an island.

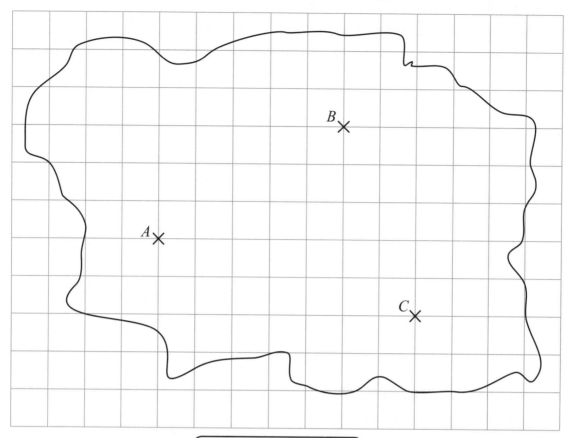

Scale: 1 cm = 10 miles

An ambulance takes a patient to hospital *A* if they are within a 30 mile radius of this hospital. Otherwise it will take the patient to hospital *B* or *C* depending on which is closer.

Sara calls from her home for an ambulance.
The ambulance takes her to hospital *B*.

Show on the map the region where Sara could live.

[Total 3 marks]

10 $p = 2^3 \times 3^2 \times 5 \times 7$ $\qquad q = \dfrac{6}{7}p \qquad r = \dfrac{4}{15}p$

Work out the highest common factor of *q* and *r*.

....

[Total 3 marks]

Paper 1 (non-calculator)

8

11 The population of Stone City is 4.2×10^5

   (a) 7.5% of the population is aged 75 or above.

       There are 6500 more women than men aged 75 or above.

       Work out the number of men aged 75 or above. Give your answer as an ordinary number.

....

[4]

   (b) The population of Deepland is 27 times that of Stone City.

       Calculate the population of Deepland.

       Give your answer in standard form correct to 2 significant figures.

....

[2]

[Total 6 marks]

6

Paper 1 (non-calculator)Paper 1 (non-calculator)

12 The diagram shows a circle A and a sector B.

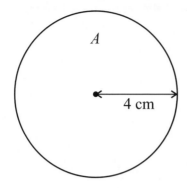
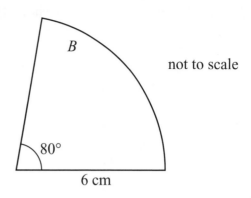

not to scale

Show that the area of A is twice the area of B.

[Total 3 marks]

13 Calculate $\left(2\frac{1}{4}\right)^{-\frac{1}{2}} \div \frac{2}{9}$

....

[Total 4 marks]

Paper 1 (non-calculator)

14 Sixty teams took part in a charity pram race in 2014.
    The cumulative frequency graph shows the times that the teams took to complete the course.

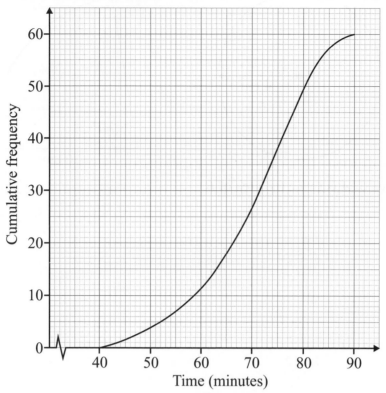

The table below summarises the times that teams took to complete the pram race in 2013.

2013 Pram Race Times	
Median	76 minutes
Interquartile range	18 minutes
Winning time	37 minutes

(a) What is the smallest possible difference between the winning times in 2013 and 2014?

.... minutes

[2]

(b) On average were the teams faster in 2013 or 2014? Explain your answer.

....

....

....

[2]

(c) Were the times more consistent in 2013 or 2014? Explain your answer.

....

....

....

[2]

[Total 6 marks]

Paper 1 (non-calculator)

15 The diagram shows the temperature, T °C, of a cup of tea m minutes after it is made.

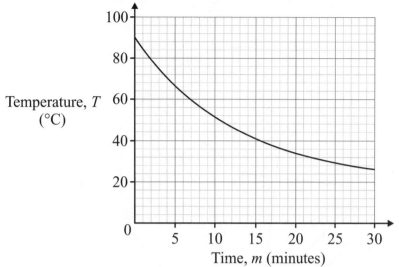

(a) Use the graph to find how long it takes for the temperature of the tea to drop to 32 °C.

.... minutes
[1]

(b) Estimate the rate at which the temperature of the tea is decreasing 10 minutes after it is made.

.... °C/minute
[3]

[Total 4 marks]

16 Write $\dfrac{6}{\sqrt{3}} + \sqrt{27}$ in the form $k\sqrt{3}$.

....
[Total 3 marks]

Paper 1 (non-calculator)

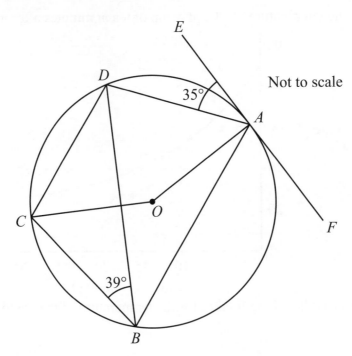

A, B, C and D are points on the circumference of a circle centre O.
EF is a tangent to the circle at A.
Angle EAD = 35° and angle DBC = 39°

Work out the size of angle DCO.
Show all of your working, some of which may be on the diagram.

[Total 5 marks]

18 Object A is accelerating. The speed, x m/s, of object A after t seconds ($t > 0$) can be found using the equation $x = \dfrac{18(s + 2t^2)}{5t}$, where s metres is the distance travelled after t seconds.

(a) Rearrange this equation to make s the subject.

$s = $ ....
[2]

(b) A second object, B, travels s metres in t seconds so that:
   • s is directly proportional to the square of t.
   • it travels 160 metres in 8 seconds.

After 6 seconds the two objects have travelled the same distance.
Calculate the value of x at this time.

$x = $ ....
[5]

[Total 7 marks]

19 (a) Expand $(n + 1)(n - 1)(n + 4)$.

....
[3]

(b) n is a positive integer.
Prove that the value of $n(n + 3)(n + 1) - (n + 1)(n - 1)(n + 4)$ is a multiple of 4.

....
[3]

[Total 6 marks]

20 The diagram shows a quadratic graph.

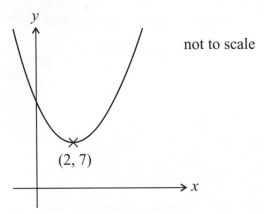

not to scale

(2, 7)

The equation of the graph can be written in the form $y = (x - a)^2 + b$
The turning point of the quadratic has coordinates (2, 7).
A point on the graph has coordinates $(k, 128)$

Calculate the two possible values of k.

$k =$ .... or $k =$ ....

[Total 4 marks]

[TOTAL FOR PAPER = 80 MARKS]

Candidate Surname	Candidate Forename(s)

Centre Number	Candidate Number	Candidate Signature

GCSE

Mathematics
Paper 2 (Calculator)

Higher Tier

Practice Paper
Time allowed: 1 hour 30 minutes

You must have:
Pen, pencil, eraser, ruler, protractor, pair of compasses.
You may use tracing paper.

You may use a calculator.

Instructions to candidates
- Use **black** ink to write your answers.
- Write your name and other details in the spaces provided above.
- Answer **all** questions in the spaces provided.
- In calculations show clearly how you worked out your answers.
- Do all rough work on the paper.
- Unless a question tells you otherwise, take the value of π to be 3.142, or use the π button on your calculator.

Information for candidates
- The marks available are given in brackets at the end of each question.
- You may get marks for method, even if your answer is incorrect.
- There are 21 questions in this paper. There are no blank pages.
- There are 80 marks available for this paper.

Get the answers
Worked solutions to this practice paper are available in PDF format, which you can print out or view on screen. To find the solutions, go to the 'Mock Exams' section of MathsBuster.

16

Answer ALL the questions.

Write your answers in the spaces provided.

You must show all of your working.

1 The length of a leaf is 11 cm to the nearest centimetre.

Put a ring around the upper bound for the length of the leaf.

11 cm   11.4 cm   11.5 cm   12 cm

[Total 1 mark]

2 The diagram shows a right-angled triangle.

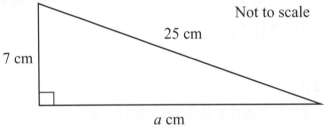

Not to scale

25 cm

7 cm

a cm

Circle the correct value of *a*.

18   24   25.96   32

[Total 1 mark]

3 Farah's teacher asks her to draw a quadrilateral with these three properties:

  • one line of symmetry
  • exactly two sides that are equal in length
  • two pairs of equal angles

Farah says, "There is no quadrilateral which has all these properties."

Draw a shape on the grid to show that Farah is wrong.

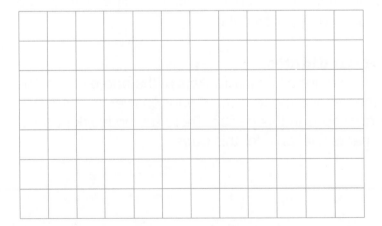

[Total 2 marks]

1

4   Calculate the value of $\dfrac{18.4 \times 2.56}{\sqrt{21.6 - 4 \times 1.55}}$. Give your answer correct to 3 significant figures.

....

[Total 2 marks]

---

5   A drawer contains ties that are coloured either red or green or white or black.
George picks a tie at random from the drawer. The table shows some of the probabilities.

Colour of tie	Red	Green	White	Black
Probability	0.35	0.20		

The drawer contains exactly twice as many black ties as white ties.

George says, "Half the ties are coloured either red or white."
Is George correct? Tick a box.

Yes ☐   No ☐

Show how you worked out your answer.

[Total 3 marks]

---

6   Ollie and Amie each have an expression.

Ollie
$(x + 4)^2 - 1$

Amie
$(x + 5)(x + 3)$

Show clearly that Ollie's expression is equivalent to Amie's expression.

[Total 3 marks]

7   The scatter graph shows the maximum power (in kW)
and the maximum speed (in km/h) of a sample of cars.

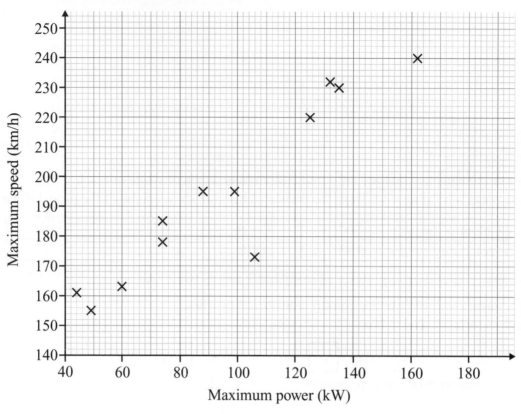

(a) One of the cars has a maximum speed of 220 km/h.
Write down the maximum power of this car.

.... kW

[1]

(b) One of the points is an outlier as it does not fit in with the trend.
Draw a ring around this point on the graph.

[1]

(c) Ignoring the outlier, describe the correlation shown on the scatter graph.

.... correlation

[1]

(d) A different car has a maximum power of 104 kW.
By drawing a suitable line on your scatter graph, estimate the maximum speed of this car.

.... km/h

[2]

(e) Explain why it may not be reliable to use the scatter graph to estimate
the maximum speed of a car with a maximum power of 190 kW.

....

....

[1]

[Total 6 marks]

8

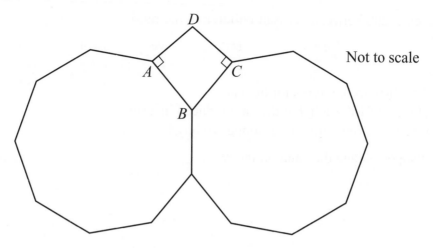

Not to scale

AB and *BC* are sides of congruent nine-sided regular polygons.
Angle *DAB* = angle *DCB* = 90°.

Calculate the size of angle *ADC*.

.... °

[Total 3 marks]

9 The functions f(x) and g(x) are shown below.

$$f(x) = \frac{x^2 + 4}{5} \qquad g(x) = 2x - 3$$

(a) Find f(6) – g(–2)

....
[2]

(b) (i) Find gf(x). Give your answer as a fraction in its simplest form.

....
[2]

(ii) Find gf(–4)

....
[1]

[Total 5 marks]

4

Paper 2 (calculator)

20

10 Annie shares £1200 between her four children in the ratio

$$\begin{array}{ccccccc} \text{Bernie} & : & \text{Cara} & : & \text{Dave} & : & \text{Erin} \\ 2 & : & 3 & : & 4 & : & 6 \end{array}$$

Erin uses her share to buy tyres for her car.
Tyres usually cost £150 each, but they are reduced in a sale.
Erin has exactly the right amount of money to buy four tyres.

Calculate the percentage discount on the tyres.

.... %

[Total 5 marks]

---

11 The diagram shows a solid aluminium cylinder and a solid silver cube.

Cylinder (aluminium)   Cube (silver)

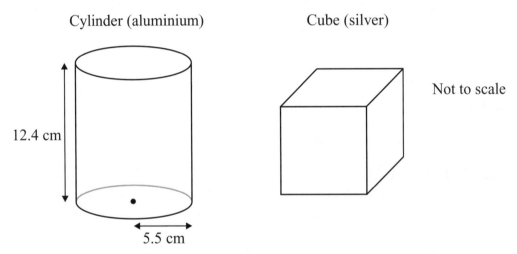

Not to scale

12.4 cm

5.5 cm

The cylinder and the cube have the same mass.
The density of aluminium is 2.7 g/cm³ and the density of silver is 10.5 g/cm³.

Calculate the side length of the cube. Give your answer correct to two significant figures.

.... cm

[Total 5 marks]

5

12 Describe fully the single transformation equivalent to

- a reflection in the line $y = x$, followed by
- a reflection in the line $y = 0$.

Use the grid to help you.

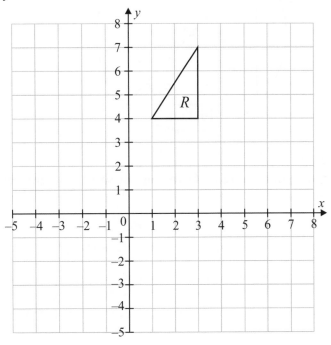

....

....

[Total 3 marks]

13 Isabel has two plant pots that are mathematically similar.

Not to scale

Height = 10 cm
Capacity = 250 ml

Height = 16 cm

Will the large plant pot hold one litre of compost? Tick a box.

Yes ☐   No ☐

Show how you worked out your answer.

[Total 3 marks]

Paper 2 (calculator)

14 *A*, *B* and *C* are points on the circumference of a circle with centre *O*.

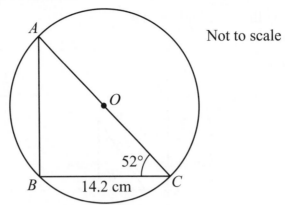

Not to scale

BC = 14.2 cm and angle *ACB* = 52°.

Calculate the circumference of the circle. Give your answer to 3 significant figures.

.... cm

[Total 4 marks]

15 A funfair stall runs a game played using this spinner. The rules of the game are shown below.

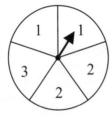

> **50p a go**
> Spin the spinner twice.
> Win £2 if your total
> score is 5 or more.

(a) Estimate the profit that the stall will make if the game is played 200 times.
     Show how you worked out your answer.

£ ....

[5]

(b) Write down one assumption that you made about the spinner when you answered part (a).

....

....

[1]

[Total 6 marks]

7

Paper 2 (calculator)

16 (a) Bayonie has £6000, which he wants to invest for three years.
He is choosing between two savings accounts which each pay compound interest.

Account 1
2.5% per annum
Fixed for 3 years

Account 2
Year 1: Interest rate 1.0%
Year 2: Interest rate 1.5%
Year 3: Interest rate 5.0%

Which account should he choose if he wants to receive the greatest
possible amount of interest? Show how you worked out your answer.

....

[4]

(b) Sally invests a sum of money in an account for two years.
The account pays 2% per annum compound interest.
She receives a total of £606 interest.

Work out the amount of money she invested initially.

£ ....

[3]

[Total 7 marks]

Paper 2 (calculator)

17 Work out the values of a and b so that

$$\frac{ax+b}{2x^2-32} \times (x^2-2x-8) = 3x+6$$

$a =$ ....

$b =$ ....

[Total 4 marks]

18 The diagram shows a patio made from a rectangle of width x m joined to a semicircle of radius x m.

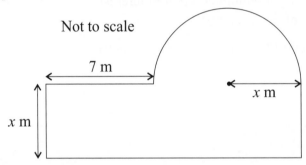

Not to scale

7 m

x m

x m

The area of the patio is 40 m².

(a) Show that x satisfies the equation $(\pi+4)x^2+14x-80=0$.

[4]

(b) Work out the value of x.

$x =$ ....

[2]

[Total 6 marks]

9

19 For each part, work out a possible equation of the curve shown by the solid line.
The curve shown by a dotted line on each grid is $y = \cos x$.

(a)

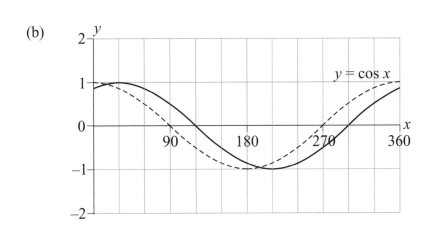

y = ...
[1]

(b)

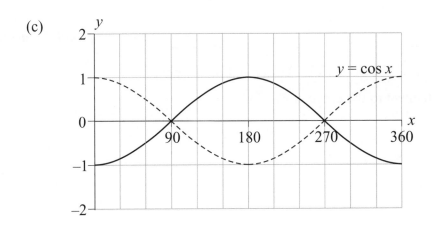

y = ...
[1]

(c)

y = ...
[1]

[Total 3 marks]

10

Paper 2 (calculator)

20 *OABC* is a parallelogram.

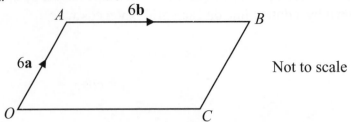

Not to scale

(a) Find the vector $\overrightarrow{AC}$.

....

[1]

When *OC* is extended, *D* is a point such that *OD* is twice *OC*.
M is the point with position vector $\overrightarrow{OM} = 4\mathbf{a}$.
N is the point on *BD* such that *BN* : *ND* = 1 : 2.

(b) Prove that *MN* is parallel to *AB*.

....

[3]

[Total 4 marks]

21 A curve has equation $x^2 + y^2 = 10$. The point *P*(3, 1) is a point on the curve.

Work out the equation of the tangent to the curve at *P*.

....

[Total 4 marks]

[TOTAL FOR PAPER = 80 MARKS]

Paper 2 (calculator)

Candidate Surname		Candidate Forename(s)	

Centre Number	Candidate Number	Candidate Signature

GCSE

Mathematics   **Higher Tier**

Paper 3 (Calculator)

Practice Paper
Time allowed: 1 hour 30 minutes

You must have:
Pen, pencil, eraser, ruler, protractor, pair of compasses.
You may use tracing paper.

You may use a calculator.

Instructions to candidates
- Use **black** ink to write your answers.
- Write your name and other details in the spaces provided above.
- Answer **all** questions in the spaces provided.
- In calculations show clearly how you worked out your answers.
- Do all rough work on the paper.
- Unless a question tells you otherwise, take the value of π to be 3.142, or use the π button on your calculator.

Information for candidates
- The marks available are given in brackets at the end of each question.
- You may get marks for method, even if your answer is incorrect.
- There are 22 questions in this paper. There are no blank pages.
- There are 80 marks available for this paper.

Get the answers

Worked solutions to this practice paper are available in PDF format, which you can print out or view on screen. To find the solutions, go to the 'Mock Exams' section of MathsBuster.

Answer ALL the questions.

Write your answers in the spaces provided.

You must show all of your working.

1   A function is represented by this number machine.

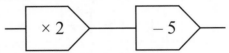

The output of the machine is 17. Circle the input.

   7   11   14.5   29

[Total 1 mark]

---

2   Phil and Samira each throw an ordinary six-sided dice once.

   Circle the probability that they both throw a number greater than 4.

   $\frac{1}{9}$ $\frac{1}{4}$ $\frac{1}{3}$ $\frac{2}{3}$

[Total 1 mark]

---

3   Natalie thinks of a whole number between 10 and 30.
   Her number is not a prime number and when she squares her number, the final digit is 1.

   What number did Natalie think of?

   ....

[Total 2 marks]

---

4   Ben has four number cards.

   | 7 | | 12 | | ? | | ? |

   His four numbers have a median value of 12 and a mean of 13.
   Work out the range of Ben's four numbers. Show how you worked out your answer.

   ....

[Total 3 marks]

1

Paper 3 (calculator)

5 The diagram shows an object made from 8 centimetre cubes.

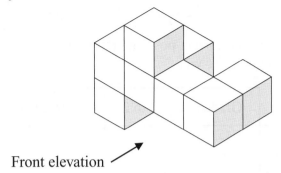

Front elevation

Draw on the grid below the plan view and the front elevation of the object.

Plan view   Front elevation

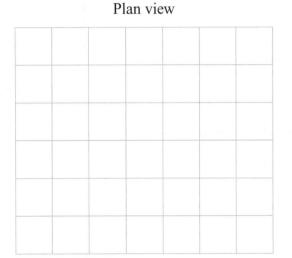   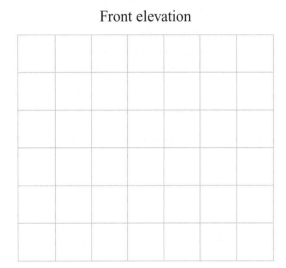

[Total 2 marks]

6 Anna and Carl both think of a sequence of numbers.

Anna's sequence

4th term = 17

Term-to-term rule is:
Add 3

Carl's sequence

Term-to-term rule is:
Add 6

The 1st term of Anna's sequence is twice the 1st term of Carl's sequence.

Work out the 5th term of Carl's sequence.

....

[Total 3 marks]

Paper 3 (calculator)

7   Here are the equations of five straight lines.

$$y = 2 \qquad 2y = x \qquad y = 2x + 1 \qquad y - 2x = -3 \qquad 3y = 2x + 2$$

Write each of the equations in the correct position in this table.
The first equation has been put in for you.

	Gradient equal to 2	Gradient not equal to 2
Passes though the point (2, 1)		
Does not pass though the point (2, 1)		$y = 2$

[Total 2 marks]

---

8   A chocolate manufacturer makes boxes of chocolates in four different sizes.

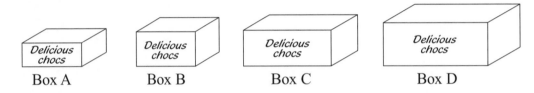

Box A   Box B   Box C   Box D

Box A contains c chocolates.
Box B contains 4 more chocolates than Box A.
Box C contains twice as many chocolates as Box B.
Box D contains 44 more chocolates than Box B.

The number of chocolates in Box D is the same as the total
number of chocolates in the other three boxes combined.

Form and solve an equation to find the number of chocolates in Box A.

.... chocolates

[Total 5 marks]

3

9 Two congruent trapeziums and two triangles fit inside a square of side 12 cm as shown.

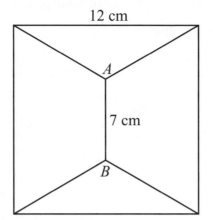

12 cm

A

7 cm

B

Not to scale

AB = 7 cm

Work out the area of each trapezium.

.... cm²

[Total 2 marks]

10 The distance between Harlow and Bath is 180 kilometres.
Dave leaves Harlow at 8.30 am and arrives in Bath at 11.30 am.
Olivia leaves Harlow at 9.00 am.
Her average speed is 12 kilometres per hour faster than Dave's.

Show that Olivia arrives in Bath at the same time as Dave.

[Total 4 marks]

4

Paper 3 (calculator)

11 A bank interviews a sample of 500 of its customers to find out whether they are satisfied with the service the bank provides. The bank has both savings and mortgage customers.

The frequency tree summarises the responses.

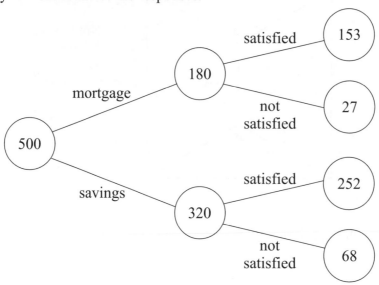

Comment on how satisfied the savings customers are in comparison with the mortgage customers. Give calculations to support your answer.

....

....

....

....

....

....

....

[Total 3 marks]

12 Simplify

(a) $(a^4)^3$

....
[1]

(b) a^0

....
[1]

(c) $3a^2b \times 2a^3b^2$

....
[2]

[Total 4 marks]

5

13 Fabian is planning to paint a large hall with a shade of green paint.
The total area he has to paint is 840 m². He needs 2 litres of green paint to cover an area of 30 m².

He makes 10 litres of the green paint by mixing:
3 litres of yellow paint, 5 litres of blue paint and 2 litres of white paint.

The total amount of paint he has available is:
18 litres of yellow paint, 27.5 litres of blue paint and 12 litres of white paint.

Show that Fabian does not have enough paint to finish the hall.

[Total 4 marks]

14 x and y satisfy these inequalities.

$$x \geq 1 \qquad y \geq \frac{x}{2} \qquad x + 2y \leq 8$$

(a) Show the region on the grid which satisfies these inequalities.

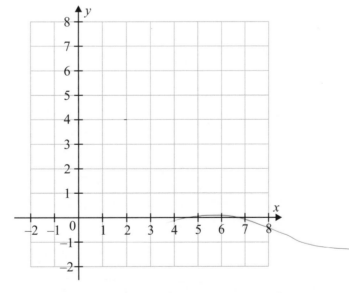

[4]

(b) How many different pairs of integer solutions satisfy all three inequalities?
Explain your answer.

....

....

....

[2]

[Total 6 marks]

Paper 3 (calculator)

34

15 *AB* and *BC* are perpendicular lines.

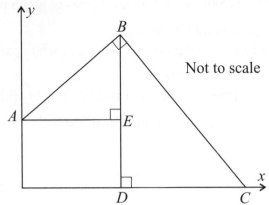

B has coordinates (12, 18).
C has coordinates (27, 0).
A is a point on the *y*-axis.

(a) Explain why triangles *AEB* and *BDC* are similar.

....

....

....

[2]

(b) Write the ratio *AE* : *BD* in its simplest form.

.... : ....

[2]

(c) Work out the coordinates of *E*.

(............. , ...)

[3]

[Total 7 marks]

7

16 The table shows some information about the ages of the adult members of a gym.

Age, A years	$18 < A \leq 20$	$20 < A \leq 25$	$25 < A \leq 30$	$30 < A \leq 40$	$40 < A \leq 60$	$60 < A \leq 70$	$70 < A \leq 90$
Frequency	18	35	40	45	50	75	40

The gym manager draws a histogram to show this information. It is incorrect.

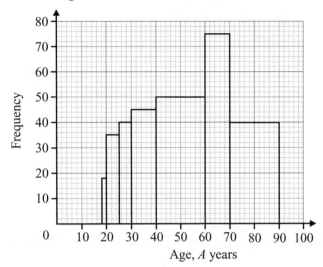

(a) Explain what error the manager has made when drawing the histogram.

....

....

[1]

(b) Draw the histogram correctly on the grid below.

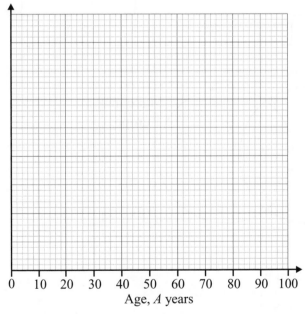

[3]

(c) The mean age of the adult members of the gym is 47 years.
Explain why the mean does not give a very typical age for the members of this gym.

....

....

[1]

[Total 5 marks]

Paper 3 (calculator)

36

17 The grid shows a quadrilateral Q.

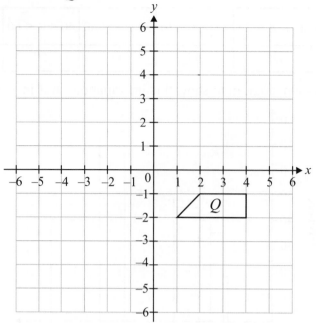

Draw the enlargement of Q using scale factor -2 and centre $(2, 0)$. Label the image R.

[Total 3 marks]

18 A museum has a collection of 200 thimbles.
The two-way table and the Venn diagram show some information about the thimbles.

	Made in Europe	Made outside Europe	Total
Antique			
Not antique			
Total		80	200

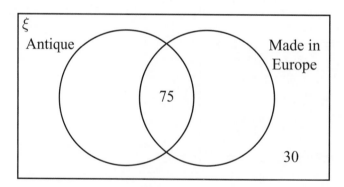

(a) Complete the table and the Venn diagram.

[3]

(b) Find the probability that a randomly chosen thimble is antique, given that it is made in Europe.

....

[2]

[Total 5 marks]

9

Paper 3 (calculator)

19 This cone is filled with water.

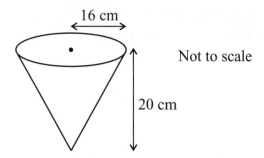

16 cm

Not to scale

20 cm

The radius of the cone is 16 cm to the nearest centimetre.
The height is 20 cm to the nearest centimetre.

Water leaks out of the bottom of the cone at a constant rate
of 0.39 litres per minute, to two significant figures.

Marion says, "The cone will definitely be empty after 15 minutes."
Is Marion correct? Tick a box.

Yes ☐   No ☐

Explain your answer.

[Total 5 marks]

20 The velocity-time graph on the right shows
the first two minutes of a car journey.

Calculate the distance the car travels
in the first two minutes of its journey.

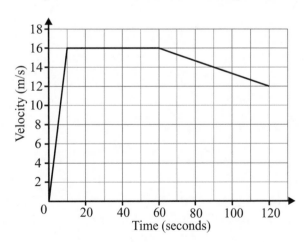

.... m

[Total 4 marks]

Paper 3 (calculator)

21 *ABC* is an isosceles triangle with *AB* = *AC* = 9 cm.
    D is the point on *AC* such that *AD* = 5 cm and *BD* = 7 cm.

    Calculate length *BC*.

Not to scale

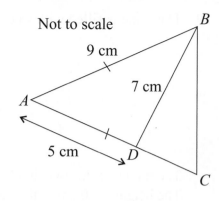

9 cm

7 cm

5 cm

.... cm

[Total 4 marks]

22 Hannah and Tim both think of a number.
    Hannah's number is negative. Tim's number is one more than Hannah's.

    They each take the reciprocal of their numbers. The sum of the reciprocals is $\frac{5}{6}$.

    Use algebra to work out Hannah's original number.

....

[Total 5 marks]

[TOTAL FOR PAPER = 80 MARKS]

Paper 3 (calculator)

42MBHQ

£4.00
(Retail Price)

www.cgpbooks.co.uk